# SHORT WALKS ON PRIVATE LAND

# Short Walks on Private Land

## SELECTED POEMS 1962-2015

### MARCUS GRANT

YOUCAXTON PUBLICATIONS

OXFORD & SHREWSBURY

# Acknowledgements

Some of these poems have previously been published
in Atlantis; Carcanet; Connexions; DCenter;
Number Two; SFO; Sprouts on Helicon;
and broadcast on BBC Radio Three

# Contents

# Prologue

## OPEN LETTER FROM THE POET AGED 18 TO HIMSELF IN 50 YEARS TIME

Sneer, sneer
with the utmost contortions
of your wasted face,
ancient man;
sneer at the fumblings,
the mumblings of an erratic youth.

Sneer, sneer
at the melancholy
loneliness of youth,
antiquity;
sneer at the hopeless
great loves and wild exuberance.

Sneer, sneer
from your thin bloodless lips
at youth's naivety,
you faggot;
but sneer if you can
at what you have instead of awkwardness.

I am
savage, old man, and know
I have what you have lost;
ah yes, you
drove a hard bargain –
for all your life you are a living death.

# Scotland

# I WILL DISCREDIT EVERY COLOR

I will discredit every color:
as my father did
one festive Saturday
blood swarming like bees
through his brain
dying among the flowers
of a bedspread: the sun
shining in curtains:
every color burns itself to death
in me and in his silent future.

## MORNING MEMORY

In the middle of the wood
beside the disused sawmill, the lake

Where I used to swim
when I was young.

Sighing for the lost fins,
discarded for ten thousand years;

Slipping through silent forests
of underwater greenery,

Sun through water
weaving a movement on my skin,

Spinning cool beneath the surface
living textured smooth and flowing;

Sighing later through the trees,
roughly rubbing water off.

Slowly falling far beneath me,
winds are blowing through the years.

## CHILDHOOD

In the sandstone house of his childhood
Where the narrow staircase
Divided one half to the attic
And darkness the other to a long
Landing and his mother's room there
As always every step was a peril.
The house filled with the noise of strangers
Round the table every chair but his
Taken and the deceptive blackness of windows
Was walls of daylight. The garden
Was a forest of tall pale flowers
And the vault's empty span.
Fatherless forbidden to laugh out and
Send rockets at the devilish stars forbidden
Silence by sanctified hands he did not
Weep or walk away. He built
Layers of hard grains against time until
Subject to the play of all weathers
His own character is a sandstone house
Shadows like sunken caverns
The warm blazon the hardness by compression
And separate particles catch some light from the sun.

## RETURN TO EDINBURGH

I think of it in rain
wide dim streets
buildings of soft stone
encrusted
lengths of journeys cold
in wind

When I take you there
dust sparkles
on the hard geometry
of streets
I am a nomad warming
myself in you

## MORNING MIST

the morning mist was a long cloak
night wore to conceal its departure

and mine

stalking at dawn from your bed
across the city to my mother's house

## THE RAVENS

down
>  *from those hills*
>  *brown in the west*
to the cold earth
>  *where this house is built*
>  *beneath the tombless sky*
came the ravens


twice
>  *I know they came*
>  *wise after the event*
first when you were away
>  *my words ringing hollow*
>  *they came down from those hills*
their flight darkened the sky


the ravens
>  *a massing of wings over the house*
>  *fens fields river the half mile to the road*
they beat the leaden air
>  *seeking support from it*
>  *their wings arched to contain it*
raucous intemperate

they came
    *the second time a fortnight later*
    *again down from those hills in the west*
you were with me
    *this time a good sign they settled on the land*
    *we saw one on each post of the fence to the road*
they stood silent as gravestones


back
    *suddenly to their hills*
    *dark in the evening*
still silent
    *never to be seen over the house again*
    *went the ravens*

## RETURN FROM A DAY'S VISIT TO THE SEA

You went and watched the withered sea.
I took you to the station
And came to collect you again
Hours later on your return.

I did not ask. You said the sea
Was spent and past bearing young. There
Was something far out drifting
Something pale. It drifted out of sight.

I could smell seaweed in your hair.
Suddenly in the harsh lights
Of an approaching car you threw your hands
Over your eyes and screamed.

Salt lingered in your pores
And the pale thing had drifted back.

## NAPIER'S BONES

On your behalf that morning
I made the round of junk shops that I knew
and others that I found looking for a set
of Napier's Bones (the earliest device
for logarithmic calculation a leather case the size
of a packet of twenty containing instead
flat rods of bone or ivory.
On these Napier with an instrument of steel
had scratched the necessary numbers. The rods
slid in and out). I had no idea
how the device could be made to yield
information nor how accurate it was.
And though I always knew what they would say
I went from shop to shop
diligently enquiring. They shook their heads. Their eyes
would not hold mine. Their hands rummaged continually
with small objects on their dusty counters. The bones
of which I spoke repeatedly
lost contact with the intricate device
Napier being dead his only bones his own.
Knowing the softness of your live white body
the commodity I asked for not to find. Your skeleton
was the streets through which I walked
the feeble trellis upon which you hung
and stiff support for all your flexibility.

## THE WOMAN IN THE LOBSTER *(extracts)*

it gouges channels in the rocks and clay
falls in streaks down the shop windows
as the bus moves off flicks diagonals away
across its brightly lighted windows
further it hangs in the carving of stones
loosens the gravel on the long narrow paths
batters the wreaths and nettles rots the bones
he watches the bus pass doesn't she wave
wonders if nettles growing on her grave
would sting much sweeter than the rest

they traveled back into the mist
while others lingered over tea and whist
and told each other what was right
they burrowed through pale faded light
from three thirty until after five
he felt so glad to be alive
and then the girl with downcast eyes
who flicks her head and smiles replies
as well she might to anybody
offers her busy unresponsive body
and as she does so swiftly says
and then of course we'll go our separate ways

# England

## EXCAVATIONS AT A SAXON CEMETERY

That trench had been cut in the summer
when the soil was like sand
and shifted loose and dry round the bones
of those skeletons (four: one male
two female known by their pelves and the last incomplete
a shoulderblade fragments of spine and ribs a skull
probably female by the lack of prominence
in the ridges round the holes for eye and ear
and by its sutures probably young) all incomplete
lacking flesh to separate the bones.
And now the trees lacking leaves
to separate the branches. We spoke quite coldly
as if the lives they led had not been ours.
Your hair I remember as a recompense for leaves
only and how you pulled it back behind your ears
because the wind would blow it in your eyes.
But ears eyes and hair are like the leaves;
teeth remain for the determining of age or to recall
that they not only ate but heard and wept
and weeping fully fleshed they died.
Our business was not with consolation.
After photography the skeletons
for safekeeping were lifted and removed.
They have left no imprint in the soil
now hardened rocklike by the year's first frost.

# TWO SILENCES: VISITING AN INSTITUTION

Two silences: the one outside was colder.
Just for one day the trees disguised themselves
With snow. Impatiently under a heavy sky
I followed the regularity of that avenue
Down past the dark bushes and the seated figures
To be greeted promptly at the ornate porch.

The silence in the ward was colder.
Even their eyes were frozen and their hands
Clapping against the rhythm of the radio
As if that noise could start to keep them warm.
The snow had lain along their bones
Too long for any abreacted thaw.

I said how much I had admired the gardens:
Their seclusion. He replied expansively
That in July the flowers were in bloom.
As if the snow hid more than leaves and sun.

# GARDENING

Gardening on a winter Sunday
our second child due tomorrow
I find beneath the spread ground elder
two peach stones
thrown there early in the summer
with no hope that they would root.

I could gather them up with the weeds
but I leave them there in the dark soil.

the mist soothes the fields
night lies in blue feathers
in the branches of trees
the air warms and softens
to the headlamps' golden arms
and darker rodents slide
eyes blazing into silence

the senses of the driving man
are the arteries from his heart

time and distance melt
with such gentle scruples
as the collision of two cars
lights a redhot brazier
to chill the glowing mist

## SO YOU SLEEP

so you sleep
deadheading the roses of night
outside the rain has stopped
even the wind
and the noise of traffic crossing the bridge
are caught in the shell of the house

roses might be knuckles
pressed against lidded eyes
the weight of sleeping birds
is a burden to the chestnut tree

what summer charred
is heavier
snow will come to sap the strength
of autumn the green stalks
still thorned but headless to the sky

## NOVEMBER SUNDAY 4PM GREENWICH

November, Sunday, at four p.m. in Greenwich
Park: they run ahead between dusk and mist,
shrill from the car, until we cannot tell
which of them are yours, which mine.
We walk together, circumstances and the fading day
protecting choice, as birds gather high in trees
where leaves are lost. We choose not to visit
the meridian, laugh, and call out directions.

They will remember the dead duck in the pond;
we, walking, apart of course, some intimate ease
between us. Autumn discharges us, as trees
their leaves – reluctance issues from the hope,
the fear of spring. Against the heliotrope,
a line of poplars flames on the horizon.

## MILLAIS; AUTUMN; MANCHESTER

Their faces   were the golden leaves
masking their grievous fall   and you
still sighed   and passed new thoughts
about their beauty.   But sadness
of spring is sharper.   Your eyes
for all their blue   will not outlast
the world they see.   Now if a tear
forms for the leaf,   it mocks
the eye it flows from.   Autumns on,
if we or you   are blind to this

(all their gaudy refuse   burnt)
each new year's green   will blast
them into cinders   in your skull;
livid as theirs   our fearful future.

## DRIVING I WOULD NOT TURN

Driving, I would not turn from the road.
Your words were your profile. Some light
from the dashboard and from southbound
vehicles set your hair blazing. I said,
laughing: I am a moral being. You agreed
without, I think, a smile. Was that
the moment the trees breathed the wind
and I held it all between head and wheel?

Weeks later, further north, approaching
my mother's house, the wind's fury
had increased. From an impenetrable sky
it hurled the year's last leaves at me
murderously. Invulnerable, I thought:
love's what sonnets are about, ah well.

## IT MAKES ME SICK

It makes me sick these words
we have avoided our condition is endemic
the terror of being told of not being told
the terror of discretion
no wonder they have loved you
so do I
saying with them the days are downing fast
and we and we have not

In separate asylums you and I
offer no comfort observe what's suffered
telling not telling and discreet say now
the means are ours the hands eyes loves
to make disposal
and to say

# VISITING TUTOR

That afternoon late from her kitchen window
he watched the ingathering of mist.
It filled hollows and spread smoothly
over the rough ground and grew tall
by the fence which marked the limit
of her land to the north.  She paused
in cooking and spoke to him something
about driving him later to the station
to catch his train home.  Watching objects
losing definition surrendering form like low rocks
to the tide or clouds to the wind he made
a vague reply.  Only the things closest
to him were familiar by then.  Simple things
like flowers bushes dustbins empty bottles
faded from function to abstraction.  And though
on several occasions through various excuses
since forgotten he had found opportunity to touch
or even kiss her lightly they both had secrets
that they meant to keep.  The mist stacked up
against the window draining certainty
from everything outside.  He did not hear her
come over.  Her voice suddenly loud said
you'll never be going back in this.  She meant
the mist which she had just noticed and
which he had grown familiar with as with
a blight.  You'll need to stay the night.
And only then he understood how loss of form
outside had shaped what happened

in the house.  The mist was the harvest
already reaped and stacked.  Already it was
spring again.  On the stove a pot perhaps
of Irish stew but memory is so diffuse
at finding symbols.  They would eat later
or not at all.  He turned away at last
from the window and she was looking at him.
He was framed in a precise rectangle of the mist.

# BROCKWELL PARK

They're burning leaves in Brockwell Park.
The smoke's in plumes above the mud
and blows between the separated trees.
It's cold today.  I left my house with nine
inflammatory poems packed in my case.
Can careful words set light to your desire?
When I return by bus this way tonight,
will I still see the bonfire burning here?

Now, when we touch each other, we
and these paper poems go up in flames.
So when you're old at last, hoarding
the embers of what's been, read these
and then your eyes (which live forever here)
ignite again before they crumble into ash.

## THE LANGHAM, LONDON, IN THE BALLROOM

Look, a bride, quite resplendent,
fussing with her nieces and her train,
hoarding already the indignation
that will carry her effortlessly
through years of lunches, dinners
no less extravagant than this.

Fast forward.  Later,
years later, after the divorce,
she'll bring her grown daughters back;
only, when she excuses herself,
they'll talk of something else.  But she
returns, returns, returns.

# Western Europe

## MALAGA

nasturtium chrysanthemum such words
opening their wombs
to him their soft petals
like the limbs of a woman he loved
once upon a summertime
in Malaga the open beach
the comfort of the words enclosing him
succulent and floral
words or domes the petals
opening to him that tight bud
sheltered by her limbs
sheltering the words
nasturtium the memory chrysanthemum

# I KNOW THE TOWN

I know the town where you lived
The addresses of three or four houses
Where at parties we crept upstairs.
So now if I pass through that town

I often choose to drive down these streets
Relishing how well I am prepared
For memories that fly up at me
Viciously like sleek angry wasps

Or else fat bees laden with honey.
But unprepared for meeting in the town I live
At an address scheduled for demolition
Another girl younger than any of us

Who looked at me and even smiled
As if she knew me as you did once.
Her eyes held the tremor of a butterfly
Instead of the drab moth of the past.

# TIRED FROM TRAVELING

Tired from traveling the girl
with an old suitcase arrived
that night.  Friend of a friend
she said.  He did not know her
and she made no demands.

Sometime hours later she crept
naked shivering to his bed
and woke him to be loved
or only held.  Her body was
like ripe apples her breasts
and her silence excited him.

She seemed happy when it was
he who wept.  Later coming
home from work he found
her formal note of thanks.
He read it guiltily like a letter
from a secret suicide.

All she had done was to travel on
her time and her body only hers.
Although he often hoped she
might return he did not know
what he would find to say to her.

# THE VISIT OF THE PIANO TUNER

You're scarcely here to play it now. Once,
it was music late at night, first thing;
you played, not perfectly, but practice might.

He bends the notes towards his will. Old
tunes in houses everywhere. The sadness,
frenzy, inconsequential memories laid bare.

The scales are not the metaphor. Other
harmonies, it seems. Your fingers poised
above the keys float like the past, like dreams.

Can melody and discord coexist? Or
else I listen from another room, waiting
in your absence for my music to resume.

## AT NEARLY DUSK

At nearly dusk
we all took our drinks out
onto the terrace
and he opened another bottle.

Dusk covers the liquid
slowly as if to protect us.

## YOU MOVED ABOUT THE HOUSE

You moved about the house, singing
Words from songs I scarcely knew;
They all described, these lines and couplets,
A love remote from me and you.

No good at songs, my lines seem listless,
Silent on paper, dislocate.
I fear you think it is the words I feel for,
And that I'm trying to talk to you too late.

These lines from songs you'd made your own
Encircled what I had to say.
You are not mine.  I am not yours.
I love you.  I cannot hope to stay.

# SAGONNE

That summer in France, day after day,
you sat at your table by the window,
flowers from the garden in a little jug.

Sometimes petals had fallen secretly
onto your work.  They lay at evening,
pink hands turned up in supplication.

One afternoon we visited the forest;
above us, oaks, slowgrowing, waiting,
their generations overwhelming time.

In the house, in the forest, watching,
because I'd loved you, I came to share
the petals' tumult, the trees' urgency.

# WITNESS

*Thursday, near Eaux-Vives*
Seeing you twice as you tell me: aslant,
looking away, and in the mirror. The word
leaps like a firecracker you have feared
for weeks to light. Watching you, I watch
it – will it fizzle out, splutter, die;
or else, in its frenzy, set all ablaze?

*Later, remembering*
I have seen you staring at underground
torrents; or softly, as sunlight
of Umbria inundated our room, wakening.
What we are witness to, are words
committed to events. In my car, parked
again in this street, canyon dark,
you lean towards me, eyes searching.

## WILD BIRD

Springtime, he said, yes, a wild bird
came here and stayed, against all expectation,
weeks.  Its presence changed my house,
my life.  No, it was not injured,
though once it had crumpled from the air.

Another question.  Of course, he said,
I considered that, but loss of freedom
is the greatest injury of all.  Surely
I told you, it was a wild bird.  Perhaps,
perhaps it will know when to return.

# GOING SKIING

Maybe you're on your way
or maybe you're returning;
maybe West Virginia, maybe
the Haute Savoie. Right there,
a turbulent stream, melt-fed,
overhung with trees not come
to leaf, and in your car,
speeding, skis on the roof,
some you love. Just a day, like
and unlike any other, strung out
on song. Hands on the wheel,
do you pull experience apart
to distinguish then and now?
Maybe anticipation, maybe the thrill
of the long downhill conquered,
maybe the understanding, right
then, that there are only so many
such days available, and yours.

# FAMOUS WINDMILLS

We'd traveled to this wedding
in Amsterdam.  They showed us
famous windmills on a blustery day.
We saw them flail the sky.  Oh, some
moved easily, as if they could turn
for ever.  Others so erratic you'd
swear their days were numbered.

At lunchtime, late, afloat,
toasting their marriage, we also
witnessed how the winds searched
for the sails' response.  Windmills
resist the time, I said.  But you
saw what would stop, continue,
after the guests have gone.

# United States

## WATCHING SUZIE SWIM IN PALO ALTO

Marked off in blue and yellow lines, the pool
mirrors sky.  These are what I'd call
serious swimmers, unsmiling, exchanging only
courtesies.  Segments of time, schedules
of undisputed space.  I'm sitting here
in shade, watching Suzie swim through sun.
She moves across this flatness in between
two elements, chopping its pale surface.

Reaching, it seems, beyond the shimmering present.
Pauses once to wave.  I know she knows
I'm watching and that I, unswimming,
share her absorption instantly.  Then.
Time's up.  They reel in ropes.  The swimmers
leave.  Empty, the pool is only water.

# KITE SONNET

Our therapist has no time for metaphors.
That's why I'd do well not to describe to her
flying our holiday kite.  How high
it soared, conquering the island air.
We'd take turns to feel the restlessness
of the unwinding line, as the kite strained
against desire.  Only sometimes it flopped
onto the beach, a rainbow among seagulls.

Then last summer, it seems, I lost it.
Was I merely careless?  The line streaming
through my fingers.  I clutched, raced across
sand and surf (useless, obviously) to watch
it speed for the horizon.  Our therapist
disapproves, but I scan the skies for it.

## WOMEN ON NANTUCKET QUESTION
## BENJAMIN BUTTON

Their tee-shirts and their perky hats, their tans
exaggerate the generations.  Contrast: those thighs
as soft and honeyed as a dream;
and those – mottled skin hangs off the bone,
hides slackly looping veins.  Apparently
same species, gender, race, both vertebrate.

Would they, if they could, live their lives
backwards, beginning as withered husks,
maturing into succulence, desired?
Would that staunch their disappointment?

## PIKE PLACE MARKET

I arrived too late; so saw
neither the crime nor the arrest.
Only the perp and her adjectives:
young, black, beautiful, defiant,
proud, terrified, detached but
horribly present.  Handcuffed,
surrounded by them, frisked,
patted down, felt up, above
it all, knowing, not knowing
what's in store.  Was this
her first time?  For sure, not theirs.

I left too early, did not see
with what further grace
she consented to procedure,
did not see how she treated those
whose pale hands expertly explored her.

## *SAVAGED NIGHLY*

Savaged nightly by his dreams,
his days remain soaked in circumstance.

Do celibates learn to steer their unconscious
away from the jagged rocks of penetration?

Last night, he watched two bloated corpses,
one male one female, weeks in the water,
putrid, of course, purple as bruises, washed
onto land at his place of work, now
balefully alive, retching, reaching
for each other, spooning on his office floor,
their every breath abomination.

                              Awake,
he fails again to recognize the errors
of his ways and his shortcomings:
his shallow, shallow wish to part your thighs
and swim heedlessly within you.

## SPRINGTIME IN THE DISTRICT

All at once the bumblebees
are everywhere (wasn't there talk
of their imminent demise?)
harassing the nubile white blossoms
which quiver in anticipation.

At the same time, across the street,
a couple, kissing, draw apart
so briefly that it scarcely counts.

## TWO SCRATCHES *(for Taylor Swift)*

Only a scratch – which is true,
not even sure how I came by it.

In your case, it was Meredith, the cat you
first loved, or so you said, no grit

in the wound, a clean line
across your precious thigh, perilously close.

Need I go further?  Fine,
the point is this, it's like a dose

response relationship.  And you'd reply:
is there any other kind?  Haha.  But, you see,

my scratch will linger, yours will defy
time: young epidermis – you; old one – me.

## CHORAL EVENSONG AT THE NATIONAL CATHEDRAL

They file in demurely, eyes downcast.
Is there a collective noun
for dentists and their hygienists?

For angels (to which choristers may aspire)
it's a host. Blake saw them
in the trees of Hyde Park. But this,
this is not a host, scarcely a flock
(as it were, of larks). On their spotless surplices
no blood of surgery or of the Lamb.

And in their deft hands, open hymnals –
the novocaine of transubstantiation.

# Further Afield

## ON THE OTHER SIDE OF THE NIGHT

Far out there

                        in this not so respectable British night

My wide-eyed islander

           you are riding your bicycle through the darkness

Calling a name

                    between the desolations that surround you

Parting your lips

                      to drink in coolness onto your memory

Straining forward

                          for the first glimpse of the town

Where I sit

                    waiting for you across these lonely miles

My islander

                  riding towards me through the silent night

## DEFENDED (NORTH ISLAND)

Defended.  His description of you.  And,
dancing, runs his fingers up and down
your back.  Like fingers, yours, at night
and morning, evacuating music
along the white spine of the instrument.
From what attacks, defended?  Your fierce
sonatas?  His humorless, close-holding
conversation?  My well-documented love?

When lately in octets like that
I have advanced upon you, you've
smiled, come out to parley, agreed,
for all your fears, to open wide.
I grant that you contain the music
that you are.  I hold what moves.

## PRIVATE ROOM (TASMANIA)

A long life
expands this woman's space to die.
I praised her private room, arrays
of family snaps (a chronicle retold
each time my eyes). But she
ignored the landscape of the past,
spoke of her present needs: pillow,
whisky, this button here.

Pressed back
against the surface of our lives, don't
turn drowned eyes towards the visitor.
Lock hands together now, lest skin
like paper never written over, tears
uselessly apart. And you, another woman,
half a world away in place and time,
can share her urgency.

## ABORIGINAL DANCERS AT BOOROOMBA

Nights stretch a long way here; night
held the valley down, pushed back the hills,
contained us. They came in from night,
blacker, five men, to dance for dollars.
The flames were mostly faded into embers.
They switched on lights. What difference
did that make to the valley? The dance
was bitter anger, leaves and plaintive cries.

And if they'd turned upon us wildly
while we clapped, possessors of the earth,
I would have sat and watched that too,
uncomprehending. They'd come as many years
as I'd come miles and it had cost them
more. The night disdained the spectacle.

# BEREZAN

Where lizards greener than the grass;
and where P P Schmidt, lieutenant
of the Black Sea Fleet, was shot
by orders of the Tsar.  Where you.

Where swallows, ignoring visitors, carve
flightpaths through military ruins.

The monument to the heroic officer
is hopeful.  The place of my death
will be a boundary between events
greater than myself.  And you

and I, apart.  Is a hero always
more or less a victim?  I turn

a shard of pottery.  Where the wind
gusts, I sit on moss-covered concrete,
occupied by your absence and aware
that history is much less than the past,

or future more than plans of kings
and lovers.  Islands, all, briefly peopled.

## IN BRAZZAVILLE, ON LEARNING OF HER SUDDEN DEATH

now you are gone it is other shocks that will remain:
    the efforts of the crabs and fish
    in the uncomfortable movement of the sea
    these too - the hardened fist of the wind
    the treacherous road that led right to the edge

# Epilogue

## FELLOW PATIENT AT THE MRI

His age was indeterminate.  I supposed that he was
older than me, but there was no reason
to think that.  From Sierra Leone, so: "How de body?"
Correct answer: "De body fine."

                                    Actually, not so;
I'd seen his scar, was painfully aware of his IV
and catheter, treasured the sad and secret smile
his grown daughter gave me (in another life,
I'd have devoured her, if she'd have had me,
our intimacy stolen from her father).  Missionary:
his occupation, not how she and I; oh, I stopped
myself right there from contemplation.

                                    She buried
herself in People and he spoke to me so quietly
that I strained to understand what he was saying
about conflict and redemption.  Was it the war
he'd managed to avoid?  Was it his daughter's
unacknowledged beauty?  Mostly it was his fear,
despite Jesus, that he was about to die.

                                    So why
did I imagine that I might share her body
when I did not, could not, share his fear?
He left, the better man, to face the spinning magnets,
whilst I, alone again, the patient part of patiently,
reached for the magazine she'd left, and this.

## GETTING AWAY WITH STUFF

So, let's be honest (though you'll say, let's not).
Forget the petty little thefts and fares unpaid.
Just list the serious stuff. There's a lot
of duplicity, downright lying, afraid
to admit the truth (substituting
self-serving fictions) betraying trust,
failing to keep promises you made. Tooting
your own horn (heavens, why not?). Must
our faults multiply and swell
once we start to justify their smell?

So pan a little gold from all that sludge
and hope it may impress the greybeard judge.

www.ingramcontent.com/pod-product-compliance
Lightning Source LLC
Chambersburg PA
CBHW060350050426
42449CB00011B/2905